CH00947239

Written by Clive Gifford.
Illustrations by Steve James.
Cover artwork based on designs by Thy Bui.

First published in Great Britain 2023 by Red Shed, part of Farshore

An imprint of HarperCollins*Publishers*
1 London Bridge Street, London SE1 9GF
www.farshore.co.uk

HarperCollins*Publishers*
Macken House, 39/40 Mayor Street Upper,
Dublin 1, D01 C9W8

Copyright © HarperCollins*Publishers* Limited 2023

ISBN 978 0 00 859527 2

Printed and bound in the UK using 100% Renewable Electricity at CPI Group (UK) Ltd.
001

A CIP catalogue record for this title is available from the British Library.

All rights reserved. No part of this publication may be reproduced,
stored in a retrieval system, or transmitted, in any form or by any means,
electronic, mechanical, photocopying, recording or otherwise, without
the prior permission of the publisher and copyright owner.

Stay safe online. Any website addresses listed in this book are correct at the time of going
to print. However, Farshore is not responsible for content hosted by third parties. Please be
aware that online content can be subject to change and websites can contain content that is
unsuitable for children. We advise that all children are supervised when using the internet.

MIX
Paper | Supporting
responsible forestry
FSC™ C007454

This book is produced from independently certified FSC™ paper
to ensure responsible forest management.

For more information visit: www.harpercollins.co.uk/green

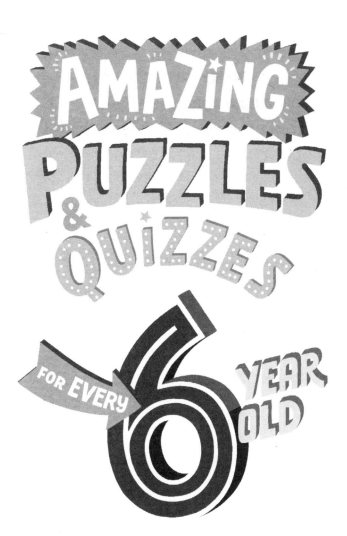

AMAZING PUZZLES & QUIZZES

FOR EVERY 6 YEAR OLD

RED SHED

Have fun cracking clues and tackling quizzes with this puzzle book.

You'll find loads of fun questions and exciting brain teasers to challenge yourself with – or you can test your friends and family for hours of fun together!

Along the way, you'll find a mix of all sorts of puzzles – spot the difference, missing letters, quizzes, mazes and more. Each puzzle has instructions at the top of the page that tell you what you need to do. Once you've got your answer, or if you get stuck, head to the back of the book to check the solution.

Let's get started!

Spot the Pair: Puppies

Only one of the labelled images on this page is identical to this puppy – the rest have small differences.

Can you work out which image is an exact match?

a)

b)

c)

d)

Spot the Difference: Under the Sea

Answers on page 77

There are six differences to spot between these two images. Can you find them all?

Fairy Tales

I. **Which fairy-tale character was bullied by her two stepsisters but got to go to the prince's ball?**

a) The Little Mermaid
b) Beauty
c) Cinderella

2. **The Big Bad Wolf could not blow the third little piggy's house down. What was the third house made of?**

a) Plastic
b) Gingerbread
c) Bricks

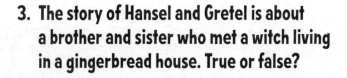

3. **The story of Hansel and Gretel is about a brother and sister who met a witch living in a gingerbread house. True or false?**

Answers on page 78

How Many Bunnies?

This family of bunnies has got into a muddle!
How many bunnies can you count
in the image below?

Habitat Match

Can you match each of these five animals to their habitats (the place where they live) on the opposite page? Each animal matches with exactly one habitat.

Penguin

Shark

Gorilla

Camel

Bat

Answers on page 78

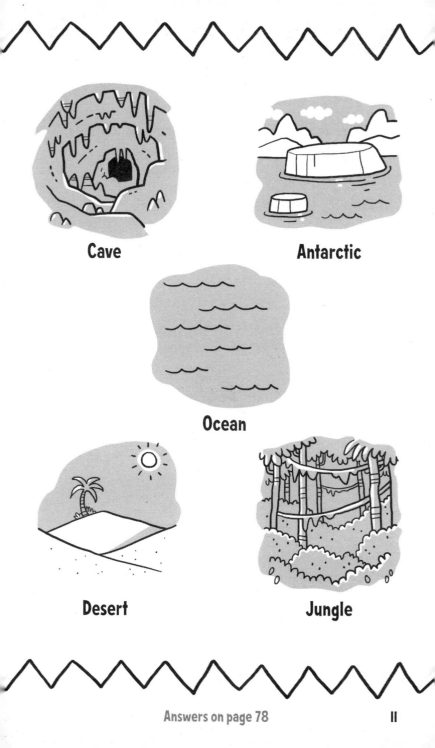

Cave

Antarctic

Ocean

Desert

Jungle

Christmas Quiz

1. **Rudolph helps Father Christmas deliver presents – but what sort of creature is Rudolph?**

a) An elf
b) A reindeer
c) A snowman

2. **Around 150 years ago, mince pies at Christmas were full of minced meat. True or false?**

3. **Which small, round vegetable is commonly eaten at Christmas dinners in the UK?**

a) Brussels sprouts
b) Radishes
c) Tomatoes

Answers on page 78

Duck Maze

Can you help the duck find her way from the start of the maze to the finish, to find her duckling?

Broken Pieces

Pickles the cat keeps pushing crockery off the shelf! Can you fix these three broken vases by pairing up the pieces that fit together exactly? Every numbered broken fragment fits with exactly one lettered fragment. The fixed vases should all look like the one on the shelf below.

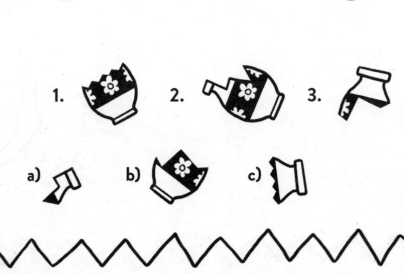

1.   2.   3.

a)   b)   c)

Answers on page 79

Wild Life

1. Octopuses have three hearts. True or false?

2. Which of these underwater creatures can grow 3-metre-long tentacles, and deliver a nasty sting?

a) Lion's mane jellyfish
b) Seahorse
c) Hammerhead shark

3. If you saw kangaroos and koalas in the wild, which country would you be in?

a) The UK
b) Australia
c) Japan

Answers on page 80

Emotion Match

Each of the sentences below describes the emotions shown on exactly one of the faces. Can you match them up?

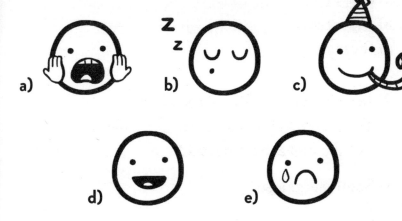

a)   b)   c)

d)   e)

1. I'm feeling happy because I had a great day at school.

2. I'm feeling sad because I lost my favourite toy.

3. I'm feeling sleepy because I had a tiring day.

4. It's my birthday, I'm feeling ready to party!

5. I'm feeling scared.

Answers on page 80

Around the World

1. **The Nile, Thames and Amazon are all types of what?**

a) Ocean
b) Mountain
c) River

2. **In which continent would you find the countries Ecuador, Brazil and Chile, and the Amazon rainforest?**

a) South America
b) Africa
c) Asia

3. **What is the name of the world's biggest hot, sandy desert?**

a) Gobi
b) Sahara
c) Namib

Answers on page 80

Minibeasts

1. **Which type of insect lives in a hive and makes honey?**

a) Bee
b) Ant
c) Cricket

2. **Where do dragonflies usually live?**

a) In hot, dry deserts
b) Close to water
c) Underground

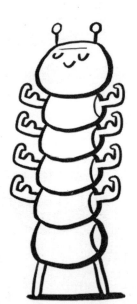

3. **Which of these creatures eventually turns into a butterfly?**

a) Caterpillar
b) Maggot
c) Tadpole

 Answers on page 80

Follow the Line: Wiggly Wool

These knitters have got their yarn in a tangle!
Can you follow the lines to work out which knitted
item of clothing belongs with which knitter?

1.

2.

3.

a)

b)

c)

Hidden Words I

Some words have other words hidden within
them – for example, the word 'SIT' is hiding in
the word 'CAMP<u>SIT</u>E'. Each of the four words
below has a 3-letter word hiding inside it.
Can you find them all? Clues are given for
each hidden word, to help you.

1. GRILLED

Clue: This is another word for 'unwell'.

2. DEPEND

Clue: A tool you can use for writing or drawing.

3. FLOWER

Clue: The opposite of high.

4. WANTED

Clue: A common type of insect.

Answers on page 81

Bee Maze

Can you help the bee find a path from the start of the maze to the finish, to find the honey?

Landmark Match

These countries and their landmarks have been mixed up! Can you pair each country below with its landmark on the opposite page?

1. **Egypt**

2. **France**

3. **United States of America**

4. **India**

Answers on page 82

Eiffel Tower

Statue of Liberty

Taj Mahal

The Great Sphinx and Great Pyramid of Giza

Spot the Difference: Football Fun

Answers on page 82

There are six differences to spot between these two images. Can you find them all?

Spot the Pair: Terrific Triceratops

Only one of the labelled images on this page is identical to this triceratops – the rest have small differences.

Can you work out which image is an exact match?

a)

b)

c)

d)

Answers on page 83

Missing Letter: Pond Creatures

In each of the sentences below is a **pond animal** that is missing a single letter. Can you work out what the five animals are? Each animal is spelled out in capital letters.

When it grows up, a tadpole will become a FOG.

A DUK has feathers and webbed feet to paddle along.

FIS live underwater and often have scales and fins.

A SNIL has a spiralling shell it can curl up in.

Small pond animals might be hunted by a long-necked, grey HERN.

Answers on page 83

Missing Words: Super Space

Each of the sentences on the opposite page is missing a word. Can you select the one correct word from the list below to complete each of the six facts? There is one word that does NOT fit in any of the sentences – can you work out which one it is?

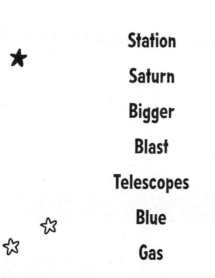

Station

Saturn

Bigger

Blast

Telescopes

Blue

Gas

1. On Mars, sunsets are the colour ▮▮▮▮▮.

2. Some astronauts live and work on the International Space ▮▮▮▮▮.

3. The planet ▮▮▮▮▮ has many rings around it.

4. The Universe is getting ▮▮▮▮▮ all the time.

5. Scientists use powerful ▮▮▮▮▮ to look at the Universe from Earth.

6. Uranus is a ▮▮▮▮▮ planet, meaning you couldn't stand up on its surface!

Reorder Puzzle: Gentle Giraffe

This giraffe is looking a little mixed up! Can you work out the correct letter order (reading from top to bottom) that would show the complete image?

Answers on page 84

Body Parts

I.   What part of your body dissolves food after you have eaten it?

a) Veins
b) Stomach
c) Windpipe

2.   What parts of your body inflate full of air when you breathe in?

a) Lungs
b) Intestines
c) Kidneys

3. What part of your body do you use to smell?

a) Your feet
b) Your nose
c) Your ears

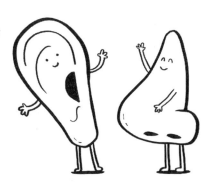

Brainy Birds

I. Hummingbirds can fly backwards.
True or false?

2. Which of these birds can grow up to 2.75 metres tall, lives in Africa and cannot fly?

a) Toucan
b) Ostrich
c) Golden eagle

3. What is a group of birds usually called?

a) A swarm
b) A herd
c) A flock

Answers on page 84

Follow the Line: Hobby Time

These kids have lost their equipment!
Can you follow the lines to work out which
item belongs with which person?

1.

2.

3.

a)

b)

c)

Jigsaw: In the Garden

A piece is missing from this jigsaw! Can you work out which of the puzzle pieces below fits exactly into the empty space on the opposite page to complete the image?

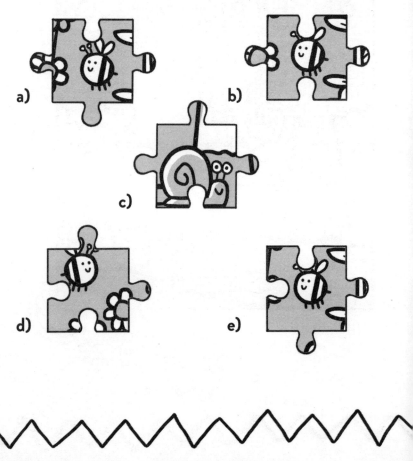

a)

b)

c)

d)

e)

Practical Pets

1. **Which type of pet has young called kittens and often sleeps for 13–16 hours a day?**

a) Guinea pig
b) Cat
c) Hamster

2. **Which of these is a HUGE breed of dog that can weigh as much as an average man?**

a) Great Dane
b) Yorkshire terrier
c) Labrador

3. **When they're happy, pet rabbits sometimes perform a hop and twist in the air, called a binky. True or false?**

Reorder Puzzle: Tractor Time

This tractor is looking a little mixed up!
Can you work out the correct letter order
(reading from left to right) that would show
the complete image?

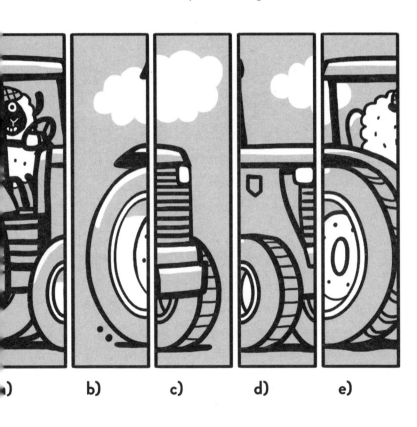

a)   b)   c)   d)   e)

Mummy Maze

Can you help the mummy find
a path through the pyramid maze
from the start to the finish?

Answers on page 86

Tree Tests

1. **Which of these words describes trees that do NOT lose their leaves in winter?**

a) Evergreen
b) Deciduous
c) Ancient

2. **What happens to the size of a tree's trunk as the tree gets older?**

a) It stays the same
b) It gets thinner
c) It gets thicker

3. **What sort of trees would you find in an orchard?**

a) Oak trees
b) Fruit trees
c) Birch trees

Pet Match

Can you match each of these five pets to their correct home on the opposite page? Each pet matches with exactly one home.

Dog

Cat

Fish

Budgie

Hamster

Answers on page 87

a)

b)

c)

d)

e)

How Many Fish?

These fish are sticking close to their shoal!
How many fish can you count in
the image below?

Answers on page 87

Missing Letter: Instruments

In each of the sentences below is a **musical instrument** that is missing a single letter.
Can you work out what the five instruments are?
Each instrument is spelled out in capital letters.

The VI◆LIN has four strings and
is played with a bow.

The T◆UMPET is a brass instrument.

A GUI◆AR can be electric or acoustic.

The RECORD◆R is played by blowing into
the top and covering holes with fingers.

The UKUL◆LE is a small stringed instrument,
often played in Hawaiian music.

Sporty Trivia

1. What do you win at the Olympics if you come second in an event?

a) A crown of olive leaves
b) A bronze medal
c) A silver medal

2. Which of these is a Winter Olympic sport?

a) High jump
b) Ski jumping
c) Skateboarding

3. The triathlon involves three different sports. True or false?

Answers on page 88

Missing Letter: Pets

All of these pets have either one or two letters missing from their name labels. Can you work out what the missing letters are to complete the names?

I. R✱T

2. MOU✱E

3. ✱UINEA P✱G

4. RA✱B✱T

5. H✱MST✱R

Garden Map

Can you work out the correct coordinates for the **garden creatures** below? To find the coordinates, trace a line from the creature across to the number next to it, then down to the letter below it – then put the letter and number together. The first coordinate is given as an example.

Example: Ladybird
A2

1. Butterfly

2. Cocoon

3. Caterpillar

Answers on page 88

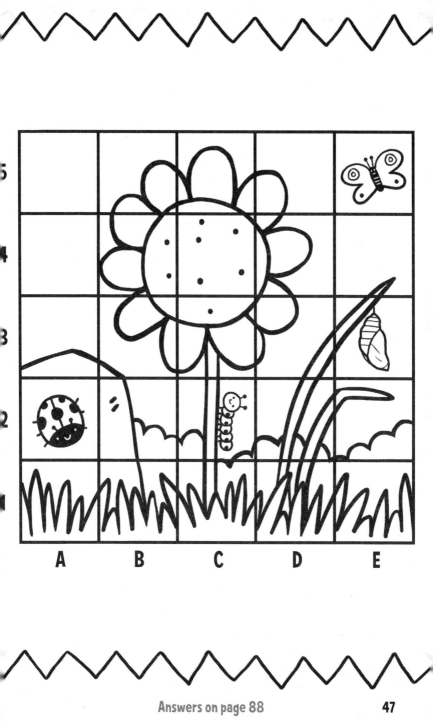

5

4

3

2

A   B   C   D   E

Dinosaurs

1. **The biggest dinosaurs in the world all ate meat. True or false?**

2. **How do most scientists think the dinosaurs died out?**

   a) A huge asteroid hit Earth
   b) They were attacked by EVEN BIGGER animals
   c) They all caught the same disease

3. **Some dinosaurs had mouths that contained up to 1,000 teeth. True or false?**

Code Breaking: Under the Sea

Below are the names of three **underwater animals**, all disguised using an alphabet code, where each letter has been replaced with a number, as shown in the grid. Can you use the grid to crack the code and reveal the animals?

A	B	C	D	E	F	G	H	I	J	K	L	M
1	16	3	4	8	6	17	21	9	10	25	12	23

N	O	P	Q	R	S	T	U	V	W	X	Y	Z
14	15	11	20	13	26	18	2	22	5	24	7	19

I. 15 3 18 15 11 2 26

2. 3 12 15 5 14 6 9 26 21

3. 4 15 12 11 21 9 14

Try making up your own code for someone to crack!

Moon Maze

Can you help the rocket find a path through this maze from the start to the finish?

Answers on page 89

Hot or Cold?

1. Seasons are the same all around the world, so wherever you are in December, it's always cold and wintery. True or false?

2. Which of these is the coldest continent on Earth?

a) Africa
b) Antarctica
c) Asia

3. Crickets (small insects) make chirping noises more often when the temperature outside is warmer. True or false?

Answers on page 90

Spot the Difference: Time for Cake!

Answers on page 90

There are six differences to spot between these two images. Can you find them all?

Blown Away

1. A fart leaves your body at around 10–12 kilometres per hour. True or false?

2. Which of these is a very cold, snowy type of storm?

a) Blizzard
b) Tornado
c) Thunderstorm

3. Which of these is a huge structure with arms that are moved around by the wind, used for making electricity?

a) Wind breaker
b) Wind sock
c) Wind turbine

Answers on page 91

Follow the Line: Parking Problems

These drivers have lost their vehicles!
Can you follow the lines to work out which
vehicle belongs with which driver?

1.

2.

3.

a)

b)

c)

Amazing Animals

1. **Which African animal is around 5–6 metres tall (more than three times as tall as the average person) and has large brown patches on its fur?**

   a) Lion
   b) Hippo
   c) Giraffe

2. **Which of these animals moves very slowly and spends most of its time hanging in trees?**

   a) Sloth
   b) Kangaroo
   c) Wolf

3. **Armadillos (mammals with leathery shells on their backs) swallow air before swimming to help keep themselves afloat. True or false?**

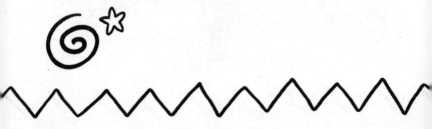

Answers on page 91

Jungle Maze

Can you help the tiger find a path through the maze from the start to the finish to find its cub?

Spot the Pair: Birthday Surprise

Only one of the labelled images on this page is identical to this cake – the rest have small differences.

Can you work out which image is an exact match?

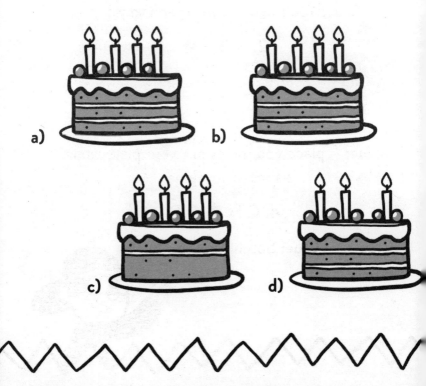

a)

b)

c)

d)

Answers on page 92

Secret Scribbler: Around the House

Someone has been up to no good and has scribbled out all the vowels (the letters A, E, I, O and U) from these **four items you might find in a house**. Can you work out what vowels are missing to identify them? A clue is given after each word to help you.

1. R ▰ G

Clue: You might find this on the floor.

2. S ▰ F ▰

Clue: A comfy place to sit and watch TV.

3. T ▰ B L ▰

Clue: A place you might put your plate while eating your dinner.

4. C H ▰ ▰ R

Clue: Something to sit on.

Follow the Line: Shoe Confusion

These people have lost their shoes!
Can you follow the lines to work out which
pair of shoes belongs with which person?

Answers on page 92

Super Sports

1. Which of these sports would you need a racquet for?

a) Football
b) Tennis
c) Netball

2. In which sport might you see people doing breaststroke, backstroke or butterfly?

a) Swimming
b) Sprinting
c) Badminton

3. Which of these sports involves two people doing a dance routine on an ice rink?

a) High jump
b) Figure skating
c) Baseball

Treasure Map

You've found a pirate's map! It includes a set of directions, starting at square A1 (labelled with an 'X'). Follow the path described in the instructions. What does the path lead to – the **ship**, the **shark**, the **pirate** or the **treasure chest**? Does the path cross anything else on the way there?

Start at A1

Up 2 squares

Right 1 square

Down 1 square

Right 2 squares

Up 3 squares

Answers on page 93

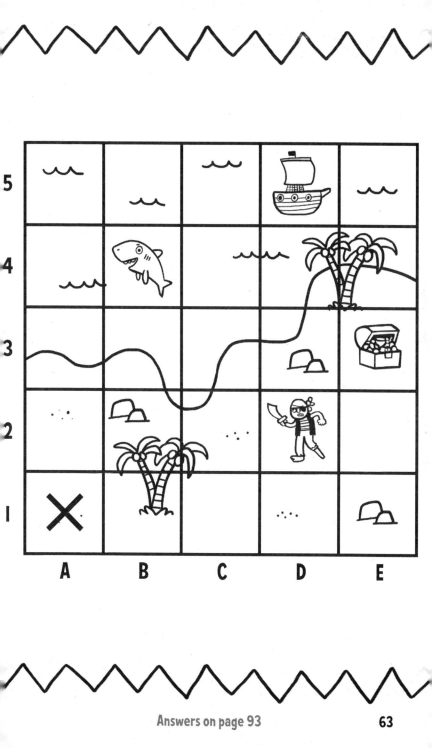

Jigsaw: Calm Countryside

A piece is missing from this jigsaw!
Can you work out which of the puzzle pieces
below fits exactly into the empty space on the
page opposite to complete the image?

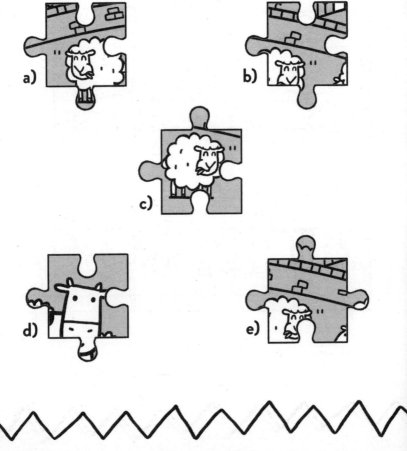

Answers on page 93

Missing Words: On the Farm

Each of the sentences on the opposite page is missing a word. Can you select the one correct word from the list below to complete each of the six facts? There is one word that does NOT fit in any of the sentences – can you work out which one it is?

Sheep

Chick

Kid

Rooster

Cows

Sty

Horse

Answers on page 93

1. Highland ▬▬▬▬ have long horns and shaggy fringes.

2. A ▬▬▬▬ is an adult male chicken.

3. You might use a saddle, bridle and stirrups when riding a ▬▬▬▬.

4. A baby goat is called a ▬▬▬▬.

5. A pig's home is sometimes called a ▬▬▬▬.

6. ▬▬▬▬ are sheared about once a year to remove their wool and keep them cool in summer.

Dino Match

Can you match the dinosaurs on the opposite page with the correct dinosaur fact?

1. This dinosaur had a very long neck and ate plants.

2. This meat-eating dinosaur had teeth strong enough to crunch bones.

3. This speedy dinosaur had a long tail and usually walked on two legs.

4. This dinosaur had three bony horns on its face.

Answers on page 94

Velociraptor

Triceratops

Tyrannosaurus

Brachiosaurus

Answers on page 94

Secret Scribbler: Vegetable Challenge

Someone has been up to no good and has scribbled out all the vowels (the letters A, E, I, O and U) from the **six types of vegetable** below. Can you work out what vowels are missing to identify them?

BR●CC●L●

C●RR●T

SP●N●CH

C●BB●G●

C●L●RY

SW●●T P●T●T●

Answers on page 94

Riddle Time!

Can you work out the answers
to these three riddles?

1. Carla had gone to a shoe shop to try on some new school shoes. She was the daughter of the person working in the shoe shop – but, that person was not her mother. Who was it?

2. What could you find in your pocket while it is completely empty?

3. What has no arms or legs, but DOES have a face and two hands?

Answers on page 94

Hidden Words 2

Some words have other words hidden within them – for example, the word 'POT' is hiding in the word 'SP<u>OT</u>TED'. Each of the four words below has a 3-letter word hiding inside it. Can you find them all? Clues are given for each hidden word, to help you.

l. GRATER

Clue: A small animal that can be kept as a pet.

2. SPEAK

Clue: A small, green vegetable.

3. NEARLY

Clue: A part of your body you use to hear.

4. BENDY

Clue: The final point of something, perhaps a race or a film.

Answers on page 95

Spot the Pair: Submarine Adventure

Only one of the labelled images on this page is identical to this submarine – the rest have small differences.

Can you work out which image is an exact match?

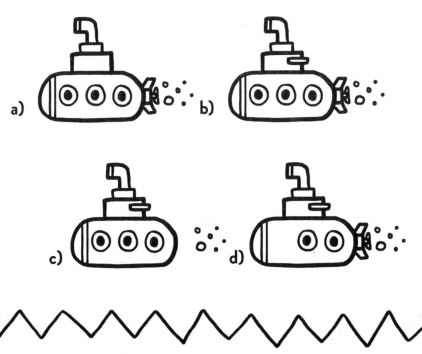

a)

b)

c)

d)

Missing Words: Epic Engines

Each of the sentences on the opposite page is missing a word. Can you select the one correct word from the list below to complete each of the six facts? There is one word that does NOT fit in any of the sentences – can you work out which one it is?

Sirens

Brakes

Two

Aeroplane

Ferry

Sails

Trailers

Answers on page 95

1. Lorries pull ▩▩▩▩▩ to carry goods such as food from place to place.

2. Ambulances, police cars and fire engines all have ▩▩▩▩▩ to warn people to get out of their way.

3. Bicycles and motorbikes both have ▩▩▩▩▩ wheels.

4. Vehicles use ▩▩▩▩▩ to stop moving.

5. A ▩▩▩▩▩ is a type of boat that carries passengers across rivers or seas.

6. The cockpit and cabin are both parts of the inside of an ▩▩▩▩▩.

SOLUTIONS

Page 5: Spot the Pair: Puppies

The matching image is **b**.

Page 6-7: Spot the Difference: Under the Sea

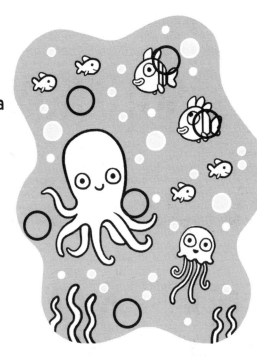

Page 8: Fairy Tales

1. c   **2.** c   **3.** True

Page 9: How Many Bunnies?

There are 15 bunnies.

Page 10–11: Habitat Match

Penguin – Antarctic
Shark – Ocean
Gorilla – Jungle
Camel – Desert
Bat – Cave

Page 12: Christmas Quiz

1. b   **2.** True   **3.** a

Page 13: Duck Maze

Start

Finish

Page 14: Broken Pieces

The pairs are: **1** and **c**, **2** and **a**, **3** and **b**

Page 15: Wild Life

1. True   **2.** a   **3.** b

Page 16: Emotion Match

1. d   **3.** b   **5.** a
2. e   **4.** c

Page 17: Around the World

1. c   **2.** a   **3.** b

Page 18: Minibeasts

1. a   **2.** b   **3.** a

Page 19: Follow the Line: Wiggly Wool

1 with **c**, **2** with **a**, **3** with **b**

Page 20: Hidden Words I

In the order they appear, the hidden words are:

1. ILL (GR<u>ILL</u>ED)
2. PEN (DE<u>PEN</u>D)
3. LOW (F<u>LOW</u>ER)
4. ANT (W<u>ANT</u>ED)

Page 21: Bee Maze

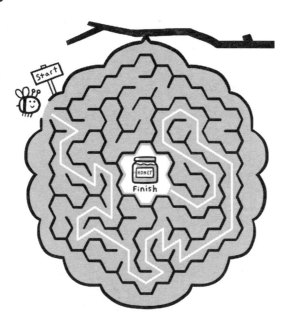

Page 22–23: Landmark Match

1. Egypt – The Great Sphinx and
   Great Pyramid of Giza
2. France – Eiffel Tower
3. United States of America – Statue of Liberty
4. India – Taj Mahal

Page 24–25:
Spot the
Difference:
Football Fun

Page 26: Spot the Pair: Terrific Triceratops

The matching image is **c**.

a)   b)   d)

Page 27: Missing Letter: Pond Creatures

In the order they appear, the animals are:
FROG
DUCK
FISH
SNAIL
HERON

Page 28-29: Missing Words: Super Space

1. Blue   **3.** Saturn   **5.** Telescopes

2. Station   **4.** Bigger   **6.** Gas

The word that is not used is **Blast**.

Page 30: Reorder Puzzle: Gentle Giraffe

The correct letter order is: **d, f, a, c, e, b**

Page 31: Body Parts

1. b   **2.** a   **3.** b

Page 32: Brainy Birds

1. True   **2.** b   **3.** c

Page 33: Follow the Line: Hobby Time

1 with **a**, **2** with **c**, **3** with **b**

Page 34-35: Jigsaw: In the Garden

The missing piece is **e**.

Page 36: Practical Pets

1. b   **2.** a   **3.** True

Page 37: Reorder Puzzle: Tractor Time

The correct letter order is: **b, e, a, d, c**

Page 38: Mummy Maze

Page 39: Tree Tests

1. a   **2.** c   **3.** b

Page 40–41: Pet Match

Dog – b
Cat – d
Fish – e
Budgie – a
Hamster – c

Page 42: How Many Fish?

There are 13 fish.

Page 43: Missing Letter: Instruments

In the order they appear, the instruments are:
VIOLIN
TRUMPET
GUITAR
RECORDER
UKULELE

Page 44: Sporty Trivia

1. c   **2.** b   **3.** True

Page 45: Missing Letter: Pets

1. RAT
2. MOUSE
3. GUINEA PIG
4. RABBIT
5. HAMSTER

Page 46–47: Garden Map

1. Butterfly – E5
2. Cocoon – E3
3. Caterpillar – C2

Page 48: Dinosaurs

1. False. Many of the largest dinosaurs were plant-eaters!
2. a
3. True

Page 49: Code Breaking: Under the Sea

1. OCTOPUS
2. CLOWNFISH
3. DOLPHIN

Page 50: Moon Maze

Page 5l: Hot or Cold?

1. False. In Australia, it's usually sunny
and warm at Christmas!

2. b

3. True

Page 52–53:
Spot the Difference:
Time for Cake!

Page 54: Blown Away

1. True   **2.** a   **3.** c

Page 55: Follow the Line: Parking Problems

1 with **b**, **2** with **a**, **3** with **c**

Page 56: Amazing Animals

1. c. Bonus fact: Giraffes can sleep standing up!
2. a
3. True

Page 57: Jungle Maze

Page 58: Spot the Pair: Birthday Surprise

The matching image is **b**.

a)

c)

d)

Page 59: Secret Scribbler: Around the House

In order, the completed words are:
RUG
SOFA
TABLE
CHAIR

Page 60: Follow the Line: Shoe Confusion

1 with **a**, **2** with **c**, **3** with **b**

Page 61: Super Sports

1. b

2. a

3. b

Page 62-63: Treasure Map

The instructions lead to the ship. On the way, the path crosses the pirate.

Page 64-65: Jigsaw: Calm Countryside

The missing piece is **b**.

Page 66-67: Missing Words: On the Farm

1. Cows   **3.** Horse   **5.** Sty
2. Rooster   **4.** Kid   **6.** Sheep

The word that's not used is **Chick**.

Page 68–69: Dino Match

1. Brachiosaurus
2. Tyrannosaurus
3. Velociraptor
4. Triceratops

Page 70: Secret Scribbler: Vegetable Challenge

In the order they appear, the vegetables are:

BROCCOLI
CARROT
SPINACH
CABBAGE
CELERY
SWEET POTATO

Page 71: Riddle Time!

1. Carla's father
2. A hole
3. A clock

Page 72: Hidden Words 2

In the order they appear, the hidden words are:

1. RAT (G<u>RAT</u>ER)
2. PEA (S<u>PEA</u>K)
3. EAR (N<u>EAR</u>LY)
4. END (B<u>END</u>Y)

Page 73: Spot the Pair: Submarine Adventure

The matching image is **b.**

a)   c)   d)

Page 74–75: Missing Words: Epic Engines

1. Trailers   **3.** Two   **5.** Ferry
2. Sirens   **4.** Brakes   **6.** Aeroplane

The word that's not used is **Sails**.

Look out for other books in the series!

KING CHARLES III

All the facts
All the fun!